NEW QUESTIONS AND ANSWERS ABOUT
DINOSAURS

SEYMOUR SIMON
ILLUSTRATED BY JENNIFER DEWEY

MORROW JUNIOR BOOKS/NEW YORK

To the American Museum of Natural History—
the wonderful place I first encountered dinosaurs
S.S.

For the Schultz
J.D.

Text copyright © 1990 by Seymour Simon
Illustrations copyright © 1990 by Jennifer Dewey
All rights reserved.
No part of this book may be reproduced
or utilized in any form or by any means,
electronic or mechanical, including
photocopying, recording or by any
information storage and retrieval system,
without permission in writing from the Publisher.
Inquiries should be addressed to
William Morrow and Company, Inc.,
105 Madison Avenue,
New York, NY 10016.
Printed in Singapore by Tien Wah Press. (1990)
1 2 3 4 5 6 7 8 9 10
Library of Congress Cataloging-in-Publication Data
Simon, Seymour.
New questions and answers about dinosaurs.
Includes index.
Summary: Explores new discoveries about dinosaurs
and answers such questions as "Were all dinosaurs
giants?" "How are dinosaurs named?" "Which was the
largest meat-eater?" and "How smart were the dinosaurs?"
1. Dinosaurs—Miscellanea—Juvenile literature.
[1. Dinosaurs.   2. Questions and answers]   I. Dewey,
Jennifer, ill.   II. Title.
QE862.D5S525 1990   567.9'1   88-36226
ISBN 0-688-08195-9
ISBN 0-688-08196-7 (lib. bdg.)

CONTENTS

WHAT ARE DINOSAURS?

Dinosaurs were a group of reptiles that first appeared about 225 million years ago. The dinosaurs lived during a period of time called the Mesozoic era, which is sometimes called the Age of Reptiles. The last of the dinosaurs died about 65 million years ago, long before the first humans appeared.

Dinosaurs were not just big, stupid animals that became extinct. Hundreds of different kinds of dinosaurs, big and small, two-legged and four-legged, meat-eaters and plant-eaters, were spread across the entire world. Dinosaurs flourished for 160 million years, more than thirty times as long as people have lived on the earth.

HOW ARE DINOSAURS DIFFERENT FROM OTHER REPTILES?

Reptiles are animals that usually have horny plates or scales covering their bodies. They have backbones and breathe air with lungs, and most of them lay eggs. Present-day reptiles include crocodiles, snakes, lizards, and turtles.

Dinosaur skeletons differ from those of other reptiles in certain ways, especially the thigh- and hipbones. Most reptiles have curved thighbones, and their hips hold their legs out at an angle. Dinosaurs had straight thighbones, and their hips held their legs directly underneath the body.

All the dinosaurs lived on land and walked with their bodies up off the ground. Some may have gone for a swim, but no dinosaur lived in water all the time. No dinosaur dragged its body like a crocodile or a snake.

WERE ALL ANCIENT REPTILES DINOSAURS?

Not every reptile that lived during the Mesozoic era was a dinosaur. Apatosaurus was a dinosaur. But Pteranodon, a flying reptile with wings the size of an airplane's, was not a dinosaur. Neither was Elasmosaurus, a forty-foot reptile that swam the oceans hunting for fish and smaller reptiles. Nor was Deinosuchus, a fifty-foot crocodile with a six-foot head that lived on land or water. Dinosaurs were only one of the many kinds of reptiles that lived in those ancient times. None of the animals shown here was a dinosaur.

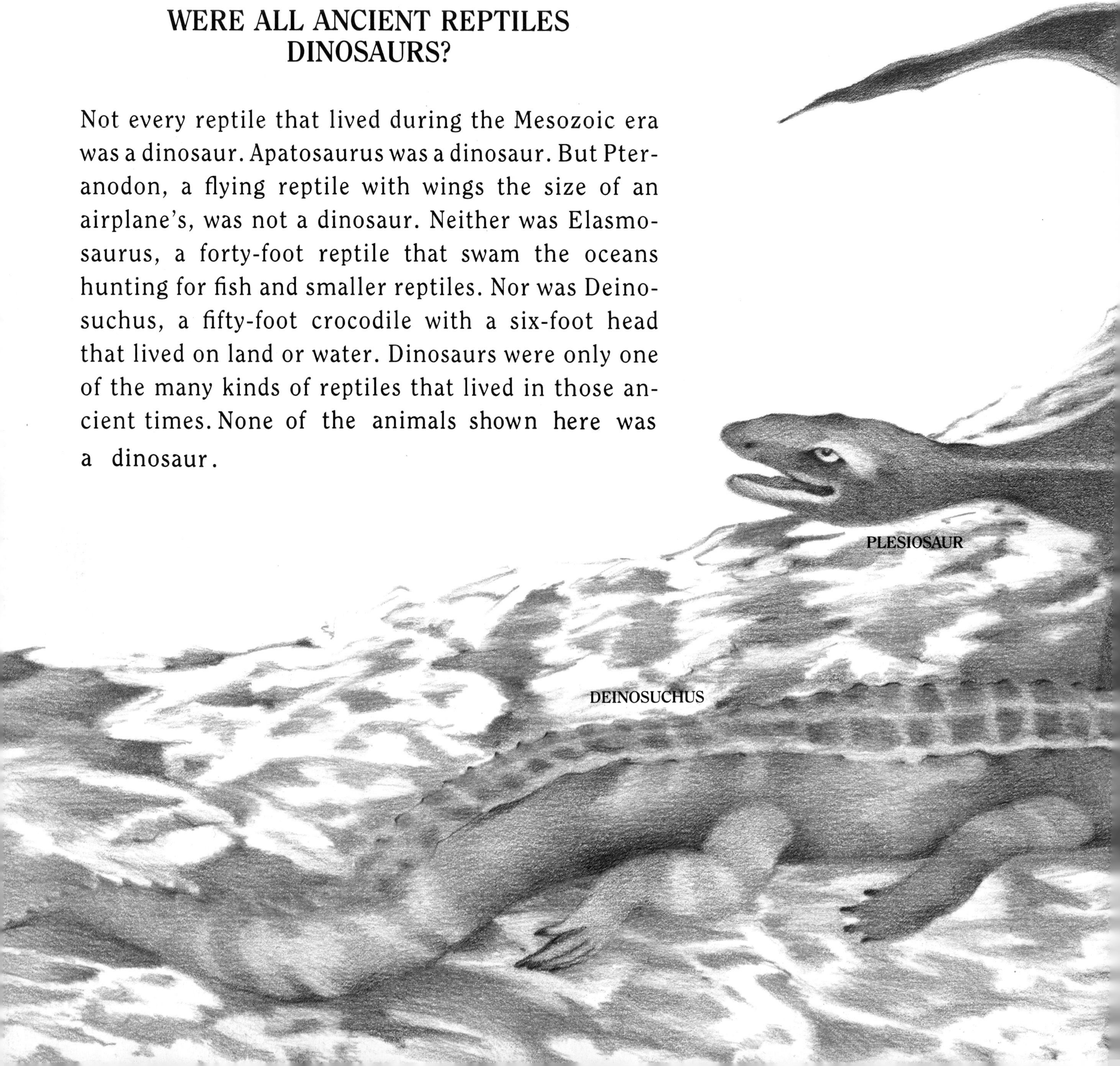

PLESIOSAUR

DEINOSUCHUS

PTERANODON

DINICHTHYS

9

DIPLODOCUS

10

WERE ALL DINOSAURS GIANTS?

Most dinosaurs were giant animals. Some, such as Tyrannosaurus, could have peered over the roof of a house. Others, such as Diplodocus, were longer than ten cars parked end to end. But not all dinosaurs were giants. Dromaeosaurus was about as tall as you are. Saltopus weighed only two pounds and was about as big as a cat.

SALTOPUS

HOW MANY DIFFERENT DINOSAURS HAVE BEEN FOUND?

It's difficult to say exactly how many different dinosaurs have been found. Early collectors often named the dinosaurs they found without checking if the skeletons were really different from those already discovered. This meant that the same kind of dinosaur might have been given two different names.

For example, a nineteenth-century collector named a huge dinosaur skeleton he had discovered Brontosaurus, the "thunder lizard." Recently it was found that another collector had already named a different skeleton of the same animal Apatosaurus, the "deceptive lizard." That name is used now because it was given first.

Today, after scientists combine all the names given to similar dinosaurs, the total is about 350 different kinds. But new ones are found every year.

YANGCHUANOSAURUS

WHERE HAVE DINOSAUR BONES BEEN FOUND?

In the early part of the nineteenth century, dinosaur bones were found in England. From the 1870s through the 1890s, American dinosaur hunters found many new kinds of dinosaurs, especially in the western states. Since that time, dinosaur remains have been found in rocks all over the world: in North and South America, in Europe, Africa, Asia, and Australia, and even in Antarctica.

In 1986, scientists from the Argentine Antarctic Institute announced the discovery of dinosaur fossils in Antarctica. Antarctica had a warm climate during the Age of Reptiles. Scientists think that dinosaurs roamed the land at that time and that their bones remain in the rocks below the thick layers of ice that now cover the continent.

China is now a center of active research on dinosaurs. Some of the new Chinese dinosaurs (nicknamed "Chinasaurs") are Omeisaurus, a forty-five-foot-long plant-eater, Yangchuanosaurus, a twenty-six-foot-tall meat-eater, and Huayangosaurus, a sixteen-foot-long stegosaur.

HUAYANGOSAURUS

HOW ELSE ARE NEW DINOSAURS DISCOVERED?

Discoveries are sometimes made not by digging in the field but by going through a museum collection of dinosaur bones. In the spring of 1988, scientists found a smaller cousin of *Tyrannosaurus rex* in the Cleveland Museum of Natural History. The skull had once been thought to belong to a different dinosaur. The new dinosaur was named Nanotyrannus, or "pygmy tyrant." The "pygmy" was seventeen feet long and weighed one thousand pounds.

In the fall of 1988, still another new dinosaur was discovered by going through a collection of bones at a museum. The dinosaur was named Denversaurus because its skull and several pieces of the bony plates that covered it were found at the Denver Museum of Natural History. Again, the pieces had once been thought to belong to a different dinosaur. Denversaurus looked like a three-ton armadillo with spikes. The twenty-foot-long spiked dinosaur was a natural enemy of *Tyrannosaurus rex*.

DENVERSAURUS

16

TYRANNOSAURUS REX

17

HOW ARE DINOSAURS NAMED?

Dinosaurs are named by the scientists who discover their bones for the first time. The long names may be difficult to read and to say because they often come from Greek or Latin words.

Some of the names describe the dinosaur in some way. Triceratops, "three-horned face," tells us that the dinosaur had three horns on its head. Corythosaurus, "helmeted lizard," had a crest like a helmet on its head. Ankylosaurus, "stiff lizard," moved stiffly, like a tank, because its body was covered with armor plates of bone and horns.

Other names describe the place where the dinosaur was discovered. Albertosaurus was found in Canada's province of Alberta. A dinosaur recently discovered near the Arctic Circle was named Arctosaurus, the "Arctic lizard."

Still other dinosaurs are named for people. Othniel Marsh of Yale University found many new dinosaurs in the late 1800s. He has two dinosaurs named after him: Othnielia and Marshosaurus.

TRICERATOPS

ANKYLOSAURUS

WHO FIRST NAMED THE DINOSAURS?

The word "dinosaur" was first used by Sir Richard Owen, a British scientist, in 1841. Owen had examined all the fossil reptiles that had been found in England up to that time. He concluded that three of the fossils were totally unlike any other fossil or living animal.

The three reptiles (Megalosaurus, Iguanodon, and Hylaeosaurus) were all very large land animals with tree-trunk-like legs that went straight down beneath their bodies. Owen realized that they belonged to an extinct group of animals. He invented a new name for them, "dinosauria," after Greek words that meant "terrible lizard."

When we talk about a particular dinosaur, we usually use the name for a small group called the genus and the name for the smallest unit, the species. For example, one dinosaur belongs to the genus Tyrannosaurus and the species rex. We call that giant meat-eating dinosaur *Tyrannosaurus rex,* the "king of the tyrant lizards."

WHICH WAS THE BIGGEST DINOSAUR?

The heaviest and the tallest dinosaur yet found is nicknamed "Ultrasaurus." It has not been given an official name because scientists are still not sure whether Ultrasaurus was just a large Brachiosaurus. The shoulder blade of Ultrasaurus was discovered in Colorado in 1979. The single bone is nine feet tall, the largest dinosaur bone ever found.

Scientists think that Ultrasaurus weighed eighty to a hundred tons, as much as twenty modern-day elephants. Its head reached fifty or sixty feet above the ground, higher than a five-story building. Ultrasaurus may be the largest land animal that ever lived on the earth.

WHICH DINOSAUR WAS THE LONGEST?

It's not clear just which of the giant dinosaurs was the longest. "Supersaurus" is the nickname of a very large dinosaur that may have been ninety or a hundred feet long and weighed seventy-five tons. Supersaurus was a plant-eater that walked on all fours. Its front legs were longer than its hind legs, and it had a long, slender neck and tail.

Bones from dinosaurs that were even longer have been discovered recently in New Mexico and Utah. The dinosaur discovered in New Mexico in 1986 has been nicknamed "Seismosaurus," or "earth-shaker lizard." Seismosaurus was one hundred twenty feet long. The bones discovered in Utah in 1988 seem to be from a dinosaur that was at least one hundred ten feet long and may have been one hundred thirty feet long. That dinosaur has not yet been named. Scientists are still working to find out more about these dinosaurs.

SUPERSAURUS

WHICH WAS THE LARGEST MEAT-EATER?

Tyrannosaurus, the "tyrant lizard," was the biggest meat-eating dinosaur. This huge and terrifying hunter measured forty feet in length, stood nineteen feet high, and weighed seven tons. If you stood next to Tyrannosaurus, you wouldn't reach to its kneecap.

Tyrannosaurus ran on its great hind legs, with its tail stretched out behind to balance its large head. Tyrannosaurus was so large and weighed so much that it probably could not run very fast.

Tyrannosaurus's massive jaws were lined with sixty sharp, seven-inch-long, jagged teeth. It may have attacked other dinosaurs by running into them with its jaws wide open. It probably also ate the flesh of dinosaurs and other lizards that had died from natural causes.

WHICH WAS THE SMALLEST DINOSAUR?

The smallest adult dinosaur whose bones have been found is named Compsognathus. Its name means "fancy-jawed." It was about the size of a chicken and was like a bird in some other ways, as well. Parts of its body were covered by feathers. Compsognathus was a swift runner that ran on its hind legs. It hunted small animals for food.

Perhaps there were even smaller dinosaurs. In 1986, scientists working in Canada found the tiny footprints of a dinosaur that may have been no bigger than a sparrow.

WHICH DINOSAUR HAD
THE BIGGEST HEAD?

Torosaurus, "piercing lizard," was a horned dinosaur that was only about twenty-five feet long, but it had the biggest head of any known land animal. Its head was nearly nine feet long, the size of a small car.

Torosaurus had a horny beak, a small horn above its nostrils, and two larger horns above its eyes. A frill of bone at the back of its head was longer than the skull itself. The frill covered the dinosaur's shoulders. Torosaurus was a cousin of Triceratops, the best-known horned dinosaur.

WHICH DINOSAUR HAD THE MOST TEETH?

Anatosaurus, "duck lizard," was a dinosaur that had a bill like a duck. But unlike a duck, Anatosaurus had plenty of teeth. One Anatosaurus skull was found to contain 1,600 teeth, more than any other dinosaur.

Scientists know a great deal about Anatosaurus. Many of its skeletons have been found in Canada and England, along with molds of its pebbly skin and even fossilized remains of the food in its stomach. Anatosaurus ate fruit, seeds, and evergreen needles. It walked on its hind legs and was about thirty feet long and about fourteen feet tall. It had a flat head without a crest. Anatosaurus was one of the last of the dinosaurs to become extinct.

WHAT COLOR WERE THE DINOSAURS?

Were dinosaurs gray or green, the way they're usually pictured? No one really knows. Only a few fossilized pieces of skin have ever been found, and any colors would have faded long ago.

We know that many present-day reptiles are gray or green. But some reptiles that live nowadays, such as certain snakes or lizards, have bright colors such as red, orange, or yellow. Some even have stripes and spots. Perhaps some dinosaurs were colored the same way. Can you imagine a dinosaur with bright yellow stripes or spots?

HOW SMART WERE THE DINOSAURS?

For many years, most people thought that dinosaurs were huge, slow-moving animals that could do little more than eat and lay eggs. It is true that the brain in a huge dinosaur was only about the size of the brain in a kitten—tiny for the size of the dinosaur's body. But dinosaurs were probably not particularly stupid.

Dinosaur skulls show us that some of the dinosaurs had bigger brains than living reptiles have and that many dinosaurs had keen senses of sight, hearing, or smell. Some dinosaurs were quick-moving, traveled in groups, and may have been warm-blooded.

WERE DINOSAURS COLD-BLOODED OR WARM-BLOODED?

Cold-blooded animals, such as snakes and lizards, cannot control their body temperature. The sun warms their bodies and the shade cools them off. Cold-blooded animals are active only when they are warm. But if they get too warm, they can die from overheating.

Warm-blooded animals, such as birds and mammals, are different. Their body temperature stays pretty much the same all the time. They produce their own body heat, and their bodies have ways of cooling down when they get too hot. Warm-blooded animals can keep active longer than cold-blooded animals.

Scientists once thought that dinosaurs were cold-blooded reptiles. But now some scientists think that at least a few dinosaurs were warm-blooded. They say that dinosaurs resembled birds in many ways. Some dinosaurs had feathers and hollow bones like birds. Some cared for their young and were as intelligent as birds. Dinosaur tracks show that some dinosaurs ran quickly for long distances, something reptiles cannot do today. Were there warm-blooded dinosaurs? Many scientists say we may never know the answer for certain.

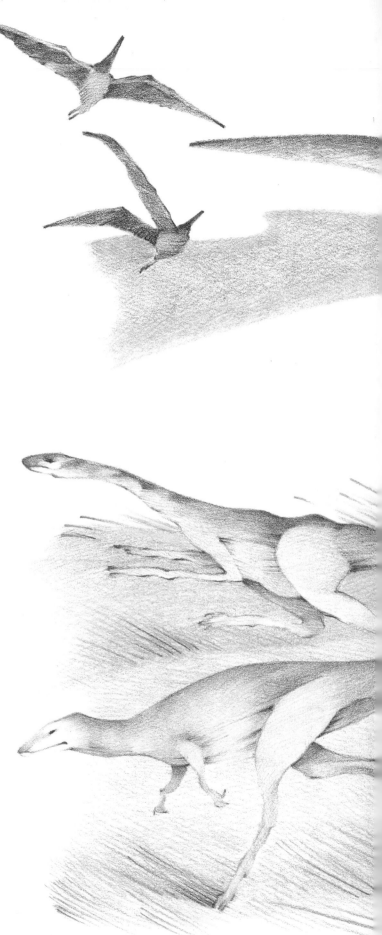

WHAT DO WE KNOW ABOUT DINOSAUR EGGS?

Many fossils of dinosaur eggs have been found, and some contain small skeletons inside. Some of the dinosaur eggs are "egg-shaped," while others are long and thin or pointed at one end. Sometimes a dozen or more eggs are found together in a nest.

You might think that dinosaur eggs were huge, but that is not the case. Small- and medium-sized dinosaurs laid chicken- or turkey-sized eggs. The largest dinosaur eggs ever found had a thin shell and were only about ten inches long. That's only about twice the size of an ostrich egg.

If giant dinosaurs had laid eggs in proportion to their sizes, the eggs would be several feet long. Eggs that big would need a very thick eggshell or they would break. But if the eggshell were that thick, the baby dinosaur would never have been able to chip its way out.

DID DINOSAURS HAVE FAMILIES?

Reptile babies are on their own from birth, but Robert T. Bakker, a scientist with the University of Colorado, thinks that some dinosaurs may have had a family life. Bakker, who supports the idea that some dinosaurs were warm-blooded, believes that Apatosaurus mothers may have cared for their young instead of leaving them to fend for themselves.

Bakker points to Apatosaurus "trackways" found in Texas and Colorado. These show many small and large footprints mixed together. The lack of any separate footprints of youngsters shows that there was a close relationship between offspring and parents, Bakker argues.

Bakker also thinks that the female Apatosaurus may have given birth to a single large young rather than laying many small eggs. He suggests that the dinosaur baby may have been the size of a pig and weighed 300 pounds. Some other scientists disagree. They say that only a finding of a fossil female dinosaur with a large youngster inside would prove Bakker's theory.

41

WHY DID THE DINOSAURS BECOME EXTINCT?

Of all the dinosaur mysteries, the greatest is why they all disappeared. For 160 million years, dinosaurs roamed the earth. Then, 65 million years ago, every dinosaur, small and large, plant-eater and meat-eater, died out.

Many other animals disappeared about the same time, including pterosaurs (flying reptiles) and plesiosaurs (giant swimming reptiles). But other animals alive at the time survived, including crocodiles, turtles, cockroaches, and even opossums. What caused so many animals to die, yet spared so many others?

There are dozens of different theories that try to explain what happened. Here are two that are the most popular nowadays. One is that as the hot center of the earth gradually cooled, continents slowly shifted, and the warm, shallow seas drained. The dinosaurs could not survive these great changes in their surroundings and they died out.

The second theory is that an asteroid or a swarm of comets crashed into the earth. The collision threw tons of dust and ash into the atmosphere, which blocked the sunlight for months or even years. Plants died in the darkness. Plant-eaters starved, and then meat-eaters died because there were no plant-eaters to feed on.

Unfortunately, none of the theories explains why some animals died but not others. For now, no one really knows why the dinosaurs became extinct.

WHAT ARE SOME NEW DISCOVERIES ABOUT DINOSAURS?

For more than a century, scientists thought there was a double row of bony plates on the back of Stegosaurus. But in 1986, scientists found evidence that Stegosaurus had only one row of plates down its back.

In 1985, a fossil of a 200-pound dinosaur the size of an ostrich was discovered in Arizona's Petrified Forest National Park. According to scientists, it is 225 million years old, the oldest dinosaur skeleton in the world and a type never before described.

Also in 1985, three kinds of dinosaur bones were discovered in Alaska, surprisingly far to the north. This area had very short hours of daylight during the winter. How the dinosaurs lived in the darkness is still a mystery.

In the last dozen years, more than fifty new kinds of dinosaurs have been discovered, and many new findings have been made about well-known dinosaurs. Scientists working in the field and in laboratories are clearing up some of the old mysteries but are still finding new puzzles to solve about these ancient animals.

INDEX

SALTOPUS

MEGALOSAURUS

HUAYANGOSAURUS

YANGCHUANOSAURUS

OMEISAURUS

COMPSOGNATHUS

LATE TRIASSIC   **EARLY JURASSIC**   **LATE JURASSIC**

APATOSAURUS

HYLAEOSAURUS

IGUANODON

OTHNIELIA

DIPLODOCUS

BRACHIOSAURUS

LATE JURASSIC

EARLY CRETACEOUS

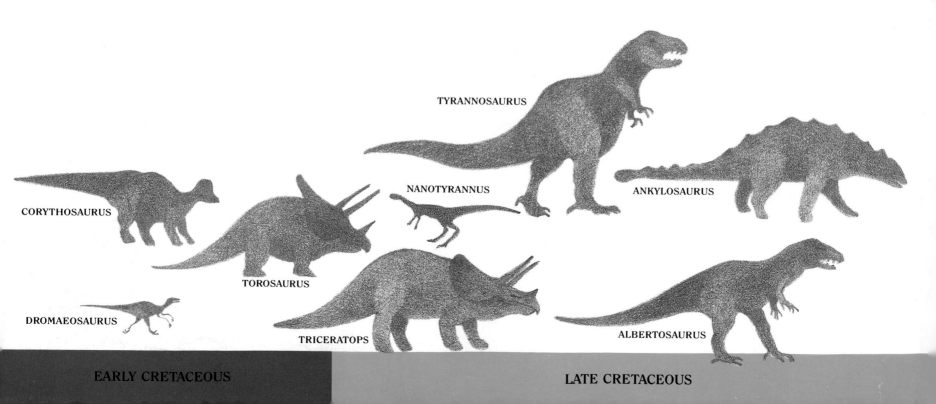

CORYTHOSAURUS

TOROSAURUS

DROMAEOSAURUS

TRICERATOPS

NANOTYRANNUS

TYRANNOSAURUS

ANKYLOSAURUS

ALBERTOSAURUS

EARLY CRETACEOUS

LATE CRETACEOUS